FESTIVE

Recipes for Advent

JULIA STIX
EVA FISCHER

murdoch books
Sydney | London

1st

WEEK OF ADVENT

Market lanes deserted by feet,

The silent houses glow, reflective,

I ponder through these little streets,

And every sight so festive.

WINTER SALAD
with bacon-wrapped prunes

SERVES 4

3 cups (150 g) lamb's lettuce or baby spinach

1 head of red chicory (witlof)

1 small radicchio

1 pomegranate

1 orange

4 tbsp honey

2 tbsp dijon mustard

2 tbsp apple juice

Juice of ½ lime

½ cup (125 ml) olive oil

Ground cinnamon

Chilli powder

Salt

Pepper

2 slices bacon

8 prunes

Trim and wash the lamb's lettuce and spin dry. Trim, wash and thinly slice the chicory and radicchio. Slice off the top of the pomegranate, score the skin with a sharp knife from top to bottom five times and carefully pull the fruit apart. Pick the seeds off the membranes, discarding the white parts. Peel and segment the orange. Arrange the prepared ingredients on a platter.

For the dressing, whisk the honey, mustard, apple juice, lime juice and olive oil, along with the cinnamon, chilli, salt and pepper to taste, very thoroughly or blend with a stick blender. Drizzle the dressing over the salad.

Cut the bacon into 8 strips. Wrap each prune with a strip of bacon. Cook in a frying pan until browned all over, turning occasionally, for about 5 minutes. Serve the bacon-wrapped prunes with the salad.

GINGERSNAP COOKIES

Combine the flour, bicarbonate of soda, salt and spices in a bowl and set aside. Whisk the butter and sugars in another large bowl until creamy, about 3 minutes. Add the egg and molasses and mix well. Add the flour mixture and gently combine to make a smooth, very soft dough. Tightly wrap the dough in plastic wrap and refrigerate it for at least 2 hours or until firm.

Preheat the oven to 180°C (350°F). Line two baking trays with baking paper.

Roll the dough into balls, about 2.5 cm (1 inch) diameter. Place the balls on the trays, leaving at least 5 cm (2 inches) between them. Bake for 10–15 minutes or until the cookies are golden brown. Remove from the oven, leaving the cookies on the trays to firm up a little, about 3–5 minutes. Transfer the cookies to a wire rack to cool completely, then store in an airtight container.

MAKES ABOUT 50

280 g (10 oz) plain (all-purpose) flour

2 tsp bicarbonate of soda (baking soda)

½ tsp salt

3 tsp ground ginger

1 tsp ground cinnamon

½ tsp ground allspice

¼ tsp ground white pepper

225 g (8 oz) butter, at room temperature

100 g (3½ oz) raw sugar

100 g (3½ oz) brown sugar

1 egg

⅓ cup (80 ml) molasses or dark, thick honey

3

WHITE CHOCOLATE CREAM
with raspberry purée

SERVES 4

200 g (7 oz) white chocolate

½ vanilla bean

1 cup (250 g) mascarpone cheese

⅓ cup (100 g) plain yoghurt

Fresh raspberries, to garnish (optional)

RASPBERRY PURÉE

2 cups (250 g) frozen raspberries

½ lemon

2 tbsp icing (confectioners') sugar

Slowly melt the white chocolate in a heatproof bowl sitting over a saucepan of simmering water. Remove from the heat and set aside to cool a little.

Split the vanilla bean lengthways and scrape the seeds into the melted chocolate. Stir in the mascarpone and yoghurt. Transfer the white chocolate cream mixture to four serving glasses, cover and refrigerate.

For the raspberry purée, set the raspberries aside to thaw a little. Wash the lemon under hot water, pat dry and finely grate the zest. Juice the lemon. Purée the raspberries, icing sugar, lemon zest and juice with a stick blender and pass the mixture through a fine sieve into a bowl.

Just before serving, top the white chocolate cream with the raspberry purée and garnish with fresh raspberries, if using.

BRUSSELS SPROUTS

with maple syrup and bacon

Preheat the oven to 200°C (400°F).

Wash and trim the brussels sprouts, then remove the outer leaves and halve lengthways. Coarsely chop the walnuts. Toss the brussels sprouts and walnuts with the olive oil in a large bowl and season with salt. Spread the mixture over a baking tray and roast for 30–40 minutes until the brussels sprouts are cooked and crisp and the walnuts are crunchy.

Meanwhile, fry the diced bacon in a large frying pan over medium heat until crisp. Add the cooked brussels sprouts and walnuts together with the maple syrup and cook for 3–5 minutes or until the syrup has thickened slightly.

SERVES 4

500 g (1 lb 2 oz) brussels sprouts

⅔ cup (80 g) walnuts

3 tbsp olive oil

Sea salt

100 g (3½ oz) bacon, diced

2 tbsp maple syrup

PUMPKIN GNOCCHI

with beetroot in sage butter

SERVES 4

1 kg (2 lb 4 oz) pumpkin (winter squash)

500 g (1 lb 2 oz) waxy potatoes

Salt

Pepper

Fresh grated nutmeg

Lemon juice

1 egg yolk

4 tbsp semolina

Plain (all-purpose) flour, for dusting

500 g (1 lb 2 oz) cooked beetroot

SAGE BUTTER

2 garlic cloves

About 20 sage leaves

2 tbsp oil

2 tsp butter

10 basil leaves

120 g (4¼ oz) shaved parmesan cheese

Preheat the oven to 200°C (400°F). Line a baking tray with baking paper. Cut the pumpkin into 6 wedges. Place them on the tray and bake for about 35 minutes.

Meanwhile, boil the potatoes in salted water until soft. Drain, set aside until cool enough to handle, then peel and mash or push through a potato ricer. Remove the pumpkin from the oven. Once it has cooled and dried out, mash the pumpkin and add it to the potato. Season with salt, pepper, nutmeg and lemon juice to taste. Add the egg yolk and semolina and gently mix with a wooden spoon to make a smooth dough. Add a little more semolina if the dough is too sticky.

Shape the dough into 2 cm (¾ inch) thick rolls, then slice them into 2 cm (¾ inch) pieces. Use floured hands to shape the pieces into balls, then gently flatten the balls with a fork. Transfer the gnocchi to a tray dusted with flour. Cook the gnocchi in batches in a saucepan of simmering salted water for 3 minutes or until they rise to the surface. Remove with a slotted spoon and set aside to cool. Dice the beetroot.

For the sage butter, halve the garlic cloves and crush them with the back of a knife. Cut the sage leaves into strips. Heat half the oil and butter in a frying pan over medium heat. Fry the garlic and sage for about 5 minutes, then transfer to a plate. Heat the remaining oil and butter and briefly fry the gnocchi. Toss the beetroot with the gnocchi, garlic and sage. Sprinkle with basil and parmesan. Serve immediately.

14

MEXICAN
HOT CHOCOLATE
with cinnamon

Heat the milk and ground cinnamon in a small saucepan over medium heat.

Once hot, finely chop the chocolate, then gradually add it to the saucepan and stir to melt. Add the sugar and salt and season with the chilli.

Pour the hot chocolate into four mugs and serve garnished with chilli and shaved chocolate.

SERVES 4

4 cups (1 litre) milk

4 pinches ground cinnamon

200 g (7 oz) dark chocolate

4 tsp white sugar

½ tsp salt

1 tsp chilli flakes, or to taste

Shaved chocolate,
for sprinkling

2nd

WEEK OF ADVENT

At their windows women lean

To lay out dazzling hand-made toys

A thousand children stand and beam

So struck they are with joy.

GINGER PUNCH

SERVES 4

4 limes

4 thumb-sized pieces of fresh ginger

½ cup (125 ml) golden rum

3 tbsp honey

Ice cubes

About 4 cups (1 litre) dry ginger ale

Juice the limes and set aside the juice. Peel and coarsely chop the ginger, then muddle in a Boston (cocktail) shaker or shake in a sealed mason jar. Add the lime juice, golden rum and honey and stir until the honey has dissolved.

Top up the shaker with ice and shake vigorously. Strain the punch into four chilled glasses and top up with ginger ale.

COCONUT MACAROONS

Preheat the oven to 160°C (320°F). Line two baking trays with baking paper.

Beat the egg whites until stiff. Gradually add the sugar and vanilla and beat until the sugar has dissolved. Finally, fold in the coconut. Use two moistened tablespoons to form the mixture into mounds and place them on the trays.

Bake the macaroons for about 20 minutes or until they are just starting to brown. Leave to cool completely, then store in an airtight container.

MAKES ABOUT 70

6 egg whites

2½ cups (550 g) white sugar

2 tsp vanilla extract

5½ cups (500 g) desiccated coconut

SALT-CRUSTED
SEA BASS
with pine nut butter

SERVES 4

*1 sea bass, cleaned
and gutted*
1 lemon
1 bunch lemon thyme
2 egg whites
2 kg (4 lb 8 oz) rock salt

PINE NUT BUTTER
⅓ cup (50 g) pine nuts
15 cherry tomatoes
1 garlic clove
150 g (5½ oz) butter

Preheat the oven to 180°C (350°F).

Rinse the fish inside and out and pat dry. Wash and thinly slice the lemon. Wash the lemon thyme, pat dry and place inside the fish, along with the lemon slices.

Whisk the egg whites until stiff. Combine with the salt and 2 tbsp water in a large bowl. Spread about half of the mixture on a baking tray, about 1 cm (¾ inch) high and a little wider and longer than the fish. Place the fish on top, cover well with the remaining salt mixture and pat it down smoothly. Bake for 40–45 minutes or until the fish is cooked through.

For the pine nut butter, coarsely chop the pine nuts. Score the tomatoes and blanch in boiling water to pop them out of their skins. Remove the seeds, then finely dice the tomatoes. Peel and bruise the garlic clove. Melt the butter in a small saucepan over medium heat. Add the garlic and cook until lightly browned. Discard the garlic. Stir in the diced tomato and chopped pine nuts and transfer the mixture to a small bowl.

Tap the salt crust all over with the back of a knife to loosen it, then carefully lift it off. Carefully lift the fish fillets from the bones and serve them with the pine nut butter.

MUSHROOM RAGOUT
with bread dumplings

Finely dice the bread roll. Transfer to a bowl. Whisk the eggs and salt to taste with the milk. Pour the mixture over the bread.

Finely chop the onion. Melt the butter in a frying pan over medium heat and sweat the onion until softened. Add the onion to the bread mixture and combine well. Leave to rest for 1 hour. Shape the mixture into a thick sausage and wrap tightly in a wet cloth napkin or clean tea towel. Tie the roll securely with twine. Bring a saucepan of salted water to the boil, add the wrapped roll and simmer gently for 40 minutes.

For the mushroom ragout, carefully clean the mushrooms. Cut any small mushrooms in half and slice any larger ones. Peel and finely dice the shallots. Heat the oil in a frying pan. Add the shallots and sweat until translucent. Add the mushrooms and fry over high heat, stirring continuously, until beginning to soften. Reduce the heat to low. Pour in the cream and simmer, uncovered, for 10 minutes. Add the parmesan just before the end of the cooking time. Season with salt and pepper. Rinse the parsley, pat dry and finely chop the leaves. Stir into the ragout.

Remove the dumpling roll from the saucepan and drain well. Unwrap and cut the roll into thick slices. Drizzle with the melted butter, sprinkle with chopped parsley and serve with the mushroom ragout.

SERVES 4

BREAD DUMPLINGS
60 g (2¼ oz) stale bread roll
2 eggs
Salt
1 cup (250 ml) milk
1 small onion
70 g (2½ oz) butter
100 g (3½ oz) butter, melted
½ bunch flat-leaf parsley

MUSHROOM RAGOUT
800 g (1 lb 12 oz) mixed mushrooms
2 French shallots
2 tbsp olive oil
200 ml (7 fl oz) single (pure) cream
½ cup (50 g) grated parmesan cheese
Salt
Pepper
½ bunch flat-leaf parsley

PANETTONE

SERVES 4

*50 g (1¾ oz) butter,
plus a little extra for the tin*

*300 ml (10½ fl oz) milk,
plus 1 tbsp milk for brushing*

*3 cups (450 g) plain
(all-purpose) flour*

80 g (2¾ oz) white sugar

1 pinch salt

20 g (¾ oz) fresh yeast

1 orange

*100 g (3½ oz) white
chocolate*

*⅓ cup (50 g) candied
orange peel*

*⅓ cup (50 g) candied
lemon peel*

*¼ cup (30 g) unsalted
pistachios*

1 egg yolk

*Icing (confectioners') sugar,
for dusting*

Heat the butter and milk in a small saucepan to melt the butter. Leave to cool. Sift the flour into a bowl. Add the sugar and salt and combine thoroughly with a wooden spoon. Make a well in the centre of the flour mixture. Crumble the yeast into the well and add 3 tbsp of the milk mixture. Cover and set aside for about 15 minutes. Add the remaining milk mixture and knead to form a smooth dough. Cover again and leave to rise for about 30 minutes in a warm place.

Wash the orange under hot water, pat dry and finely grate the zest. Coarsely chop the white chocolate, candied orange and lemon peel and pistachios. Combine the mixture with the orange zest. Vigorously knead the dough, incorporating the pistachio mixture.

Grease a panettone tin (or a small kugelhopf tin). Transfer the dough to the tin, cover and leave to rise for about 15 minutes. Preheat the oven to 180°C (350°F). Bake the panettone on the middle rack for about 30 minutes. Whisk the egg yolk into the extra milk and brush it over the cake. Continue to bake the panettone for another 15 minutes on the lowest rack. Remove from the oven and leave to cool. Dust generously with icing sugar to serve.

STUFFED WITLOF

Core and finely dice the apples. Combine the apple in a bowl with the grated parmesan, cream cheese and lemon juice. Thinly slice the smoked salmon and add it to the apple mixture. Season with salt and pepper.

Coarsely chop the walnuts and dry-roast in a frying pan.

Cut the witlof heads in half lengthways, then wash and pat dry. Arrange the witlof halves on a plate. Divide the filling among the witlof and garnish with the walnuts.

SERVES 4

2 apples

½ cup (50 g) grated parmesan cheese

75 g (2½ oz) cream cheese

2 tbsp lemon juice

100 g (3½ oz) smoked salmon

Salt

Pepper

1 cup (115 g) walnuts

2 large heads of chicory (witlof)

3rd

WEEK OF ADVENT

And I go beyond the village gates

Into fields beyond the paths,

Divine radiance, sublime state!

So silent the world, so vast!

PUMPKIN WELLINGTONS
with kale pesto and beetroot

SERVES 4

1 red onion

250 g (9 oz) beetroot

½ butternut pumpkin (squash)

5 garlic cloves

2 tbsp olive oil

1 tbsp thyme, plus a little extra for garnish

1 tbsp sumac, plus a little extra for garnish

250 g (9 oz) cooked Puy lentils

Sea salt

550 g (1 lb 4 oz) puff pastry sheets

2 tbsp almond milk

KALE PESTO

180 g (6 oz) cooked chestnuts

½ lemon

100 g (3½ oz) kale

4 tbsp olive oil

Preheat the oven to 190°C (375°F). Peel the onion and cut it into eight wedges. Peel and dice the beetroot. Peel and dice the pumpkin. Bruise the garlic cloves, leaving the skins on. Transfer the vegetables to a bowl and toss with the garlic, olive oil, thyme and sumac. Spread the mixture over a baking tray and roast for 45 minutes. Peel and mash the garlic. Transfer the vegetables to a bowl, add the lentils and stir in half of the mashed garlic. Season with salt and leave to cool.

For the pesto, coarsely chop the chestnuts. Juice the lemon. Blanch the kale in boiling water, then drain and squeeze to remove excess water. Combine the chestnuts, kale and lemon juice with the remaining roasted garlic, olive oil and a little salt. Blend to form a thick pesto.

Trim the pastry to make four rectangles, about 19 x 25 cm (7½ x 10 inches) each (join the sheets together if needed). Spread half of each rectangle with the pesto and top with the lentil filling. Brush the edges with almond milk, fold the other half over and press the edges together to seal. Transfer the Wellingtons to a baking tray lined with baking paper and chill for 1 hour.

Preheat the oven to 190°C (375°F). Brush the Wellingtons with almond milk, sprinkle with sumac and bake for about 30–40 minutes or until golden brown. Sprinkle with a little thyme and sea salt just before serving.

JAM COOKIES

Sift the flour and icing sugar into a large bowl and sprinkle the white sugar and cinnamon on top. Dice the butter and add it to the mixture along with the egg yolks and vanilla. Knead until the dough is well combined. Shape it into a ball, wrap in plastic wrap and refrigerate for 30 minutes.

Preheat the oven to 180°C (350°F). Line two baking trays with baking paper.

Roll out the dough until 3 mm (⅛ inch) thick. Cut an even number of circles from the dough using a round cookie cutter. Cut a 1 cm (½ inch) hole in the centre of half of the cookies. Transfer all the cookies to the trays and bake until golden brown, about 10 minutes.

Meanwhile, heat the jam and rum in a small saucepan and stir until smooth. Remove the cookies from the trays while still hot. Spread those without holes with ½ tsp of the jam mixture. Top with a cookie with a hole cut in it and sprinkle with icing sugar. Once cooled, store in an airtight container.

MAKES ABOUT 40

2 cups (300 g) plain (all-purpose) flour

100 g (3½ oz) icing (confectioners') sugar, plus extra for dusting

1½ tbsp white sugar

1 pinch ground cinnamon

200 g (7 oz) butter, at room temperature

2 egg yolks

1 tsp vanilla extract

¾ cup (250 g) blackcurrant jam

2 tbsp rum

15

SAFFRON & CINNAMON RING

MAKES AN 18 CM (7 INCH) RING

12 g (¼ oz) fresh yeast

40 g (1½ oz) butter

½ cup (125 ml) milk, plus 2 tbsp milk for brushing

1 small pinch saffron threads

25 g (1 oz) raw sugar

¼ tsp salt

½ tsp ground cardamom

1⅓ cups (200 g) spelt flour, plus extra for dusting

1 egg, for glazing

CINNAMON FILLING

50 g (1¾ oz) butter, at room temperature

25 g (1 oz) raw sugar

½ tsp ground cinnamon

¼ tsp vanilla bean paste

Grated zest of ½ orange

1 pinch salt

Crumble the yeast into a large bowl. Melt the butter in a small saucepan, add the milk and saffron, and heat until lukewarm. Pour the mixture over the yeast and stir until the yeast has dissolved. Stir in the sugar, salt, cardamom and flour. Knead for at least 5 minutes to make a smooth, pliable dough. Cover the bowl and set the dough aside to rest for 60–90 minutes or until it has doubled in volume.

Meanwhile, combine all of the ingredients for the filling in a small bowl and set aside.

Lightly dust your benchtop with flour and roll out the risen dough to a 50 x 30 cm (20 x 12 inch) rectangle. Spread the filling mixture over the dough, leaving an edge of about 1 cm (½ inch). Roll the dough up from the long side. Use a sharp knife to cut the rolled-up dough in half lengthways to make two long pieces. Turn the cut surfaces up and twist the two pieces into a plait, ensuring that the cut surfaces (showing the filling) face upwards.

Preheat the oven to 200°C (400°F). Transfer the plait to a baking tray lined with baking paper and shape it into a ring by connecting the two ends. Loosely cover the ring and leave it to rise again for 45 minutes. Whisk the egg and milk and brush it over the ring. Bake until golden brown, about 18 minutes. Leave to cool a little on a wire rack.

16

BRAISED FENNEL
with tomatoes and pastis

Wash and trim the fennel bulbs, reserving the green fronds. Remove the core. Slice the bulbs into eight wedges. Peel and finely chop the garlic and shallots. Wash the thyme and pat it dry. Pick off the leaves.

Heat the oil in a frying pan. Add the fennel and fennel seeds and sear. Add the shallots and thyme and fry briefly. Stir in the garlic, then add the tomatoes. Deglaze the pan with the wine and pastis. Season with sugar, salt and pepper. Reduce the heat to low, cover and simmer for 20 minutes.

Divide the fennel mixture among four serving plates. Tear the reserved fennel fronds into small pieces and sprinkle them over the top. Serve with a crusty baguette.

SERVES 4

1 kg (2 lb 4 oz) fennel

4 garlic cloves

2 French shallots

5 sprigs thyme

4 tbsp olive oil

2 tsp fennel seeds

200 g (7 oz) tinned diced tomatoes

⅓ cup (80 ml) dry white wine or vegetable stock

3 tbsp pastis

1 pinch white sugar

Salt

Pepper

Crusty baguette, to serve

PEAR PUNCH

SERVES 4

4 fruit infusion teabags
2 cinnamon sticks
1 pear
1 lemon
350 ml (12 fl oz) white wine
¼ cup (55 g) raw sugar
100 ml (3½ fl oz) rum

Bring 2 cups (500 ml) water to the boil in a small saucepan. Add the teabags and cinnamon sticks and set aside to steep for 5–8 minutes.

Meanwhile, peel the pear and cut it into quarters, removing the core, then finely dice. Rinse the lemon under hot water and pat dry. Use a vegetable peeler to slice off the zest in a long spiral. Juice the lemon.

Stir the white wine, lemon peel, lemon juice, sugar and rum into the tea. Reheat, stirring until the sugar has dissolved. Spoon the diced pear into four glasses and strain the punch over the top.

ROSEMARY &
LEMON FRIANDS

Preheat the oven to 190°C (375°F). Butter the holes of a muffin tin and dust with flour.

Sift the flour, baking powder and icing sugar into a bowl and mix in the ground almonds. In another bowl, beat the egg whites with the salt until stiff. Add to the dry ingredients along with the oil, honey and lemon zest and fold in gently. Fill the holes of the muffin tin about three-quarters full with the batter. Sprinkle with the flaked almonds and bake the friands for 15–20 minutes.

Meanwhile, for the syrup, wash the lemons under hot water. Pat dry, peel and slice the peel into fine strips. Juice the lemons. Rinse and the rosemary sprigs and pat dry.

Briefly blanch the lemon peel strips. Add the lemon peel, lemon juice, rosemary sprigs, sugar and ⅓ cup (80 ml) water to a small saucepan. Bring to the boil, reduce the heat and simmer until reduced by half. Remove the rosemary sprigs.

Remove the friands from the tin and set aside to cool a little on a wire rack. Drizzle the syrup, including the lemon zest, over the warm friands. Serve warm.

MAKES 12

Butter, for greasing

½ cup (75 g) plain (all-purpose) flour, plus extra for dusting

½ tsp baking powder

1¼ cups (150 g) icing (confectioners') sugar

1¼ cups (125 g) ground almonds

3 egg whites

1 pinch salt

½ cup (125 ml) olive oil

1 tsp honey

Zest of 2 lemons, grated

3 tbsp flaked almonds

ROSEMARY SYRUP

2 lemons

2 sprigs rosemary

100 g (3½ oz) white sugar

4th

WEEK OF ADVENT

The distant arc of stars is long,

From the snow of desolation

Rising wonderfully like song –

O merciful occasion!

CRANBERRY SHORTBREAD

MAKES ABOUT 40

⅔ cup (100 g) dried cranberries

2 cups (300 g) plain (all-purpose) flour

200 g (7 oz) chilled salted butter

100 g (3½ oz) white sugar

2 tsp vanilla extract

Preheat the oven to 180°C (350°F). Line two baking trays with baking paper.

Finely chop the cranberries. Sift the flour into a bowl. Rub in the butter with your fingertips until the mixture resembles breadcrumbs. Stir in the sugar, cranberries and vanilla. Press the dough into a ball. Wrap in plastic and refrigerate for 15 minutes.

Roll out the dough until 3 mm (⅛ inch) thick. Cut circles from the dough using a round cookie cutter. Transfer the cookies to the trays and bake for about 15 minutes or until just starting to brown. Carefully remove the cookies from the trays and leave to cool on a wire rack. Store in an airtight container.

TIP: KNEAD THE DOUGH AS LITTLE AS POSSIBLE TO KEEP THIS DELICIOUS, BUTTERY SHORTBREAD LIGHT AND SHORT.

LEG OF LAMB
with soft goat's cheese and herb salad

Rinse the oregano, pat dry and pick off the leaves. Peel the garlic. Combine the oregano, garlic, lemon zest, salt and 1 tbsp of the olive oil. Pound the mixture to a paste using a mortar and pestle. Add the remaining oil and mix well.

Pierce the leg of lamb all over with the tip of a sharp knife and rub with the herb paste. Transfer to a large resealable plastic bag, seal tightly and leave to marinate in the refrigerator for at least 3 hours or overnight, turning occasionally.

Remove the lamb from the refrigerator and allow it to come to room temperature. Preheat the oven grill (broiler) to the highest setting. Cook the lamb for 15 minutes each side, then set aside to rest for 10 minutes.

For the salad, wash the herbs and rocket, then shake or spin dry. Chop coarsely and place in a bowl. Combine with olive oil and lemon juice, to taste. Season with salt and pepper.

Thickly slice the lamb and serve it with the herb salad and crumbled goat's cheese.

SERVES 4

1 bunch oregano

5 garlic cloves

Zest of 2 lemons, grated

1 tsp sea salt

90 ml (3 fl oz) olive oil

½ leg of lamb (deboned and butterflied)

200 g (7 oz) soft goat's cheese

HERB SALAD

2 bunches of herbs, e.g. basil, mint, coriander (cilantro) or parsley

1 cup (50 g) rocket

Olive oil

Juice of 1 lemon

Salt

Pepper

PANNA COTTA
with caramel sauce

SERVES 4

200 ml (7 fl oz) milk

400 ml (14 fl oz) single (pure) cream

¾ cup (160 g) white sugar

1 vanilla bean

3 gelatine leaves

Add the milk, cream and ¼ cup (50 g) of the sugar to a saucepan. Split the vanilla bean lengthways and scrape the seeds into the pan. Add the empty pod. Simmer over low heat for about 15 minutes. Remove from the heat.

Rinse four small ramekins with water. Add the remaining sugar to a small saucepan and caramelise over medium heat until melted and golden brown. Stir in 2 tbsp water and whisk until the mixture comes away from the side of the pan. Divide the caramel evenly among the ramekins.

Soak the gelatine in cold water for about 5 minutes, then squeeze out the excess water. Remove the vanilla pod from the cream mixture. Add the gelatine and stir to dissolve. Divide the mixture evenly among the ramekins. Leave to cool to room temperature, then transfer to the refrigerator to firm up for at least 3 hours, preferably overnight.

To serve, briefly stand the ramekins in hot water to loosen the panna cotta. If necessary, run a sharp knife around the insides of the ramekins. Invert the panna cotta onto dessert plates and serve.

TIP: SERVE TOPPED WITH BERRIES.

MULLED WINE

with cumquats

Heat the red wine, sugar, vanilla and spices in a saucepan over low heat.

Meanwhile, rinse the cumquats under hot water, slice and divide among four glasses.

Strain the mulled wine. Serve immediately into the glasses.

SERVES 4

1 bottle red wine

100 g (3½ oz) white sugar

1 teaspoon vanilla extract

2 star anise

1 cinnamon stick

6 cloves

8 cumquats

SALMON & POTATOES
with pea pesto

SERVES 4

400 g (14 oz) waxy potatoes

Salt

4 salmon fillets

Smoked salt

1 small lemon

8 small sprigs lemon thyme

2 tbsp butter

PEA PESTO

1¼ cups (180 g) frozen peas

1 garlic clove, peeled

⅓ cup (50 g) pine nuts

½ cup (50 g) grated parmesan cheese

3 tbsp olive oil

Salt

Pepper

Preheat the oven to 140°C (275°F).

Wash and peel the potatoes and boil in salted water for about 20 minutes.

Meanwhile, rinse the salmon fillets under cold water and pat dry. Place each fillet on a piece of baking paper and season with smoked salt. Wash the lemon under hot water, pat dry and slice thinly. Place the lemon slices on top of the salmon fillets. Rinse the thyme, pat dry and sprinkle over the salmon. Dot with the butter. Wrap up the parcels and seal with twine. Place in a baking dish or on a tray and bake for about 20 minutes.

For the pesto, blanch the peas in boiling salted water for 4–5 minutes, then refresh under cold water. Transfer the peas, garlic, pine nuts, parmesan and olive oil to a tall beaker. Use a stick blender to blend until creamy, then season with salt and pepper.

Remove the fish from the oven and serve with the potatoes and pea pesto.

CREAMY PARSNIP SOUP
with thyme croutons

Peel and dice the shallot. Peel and slice the parsnips. Heat the olive oil in a saucepan. Add the shallot and parsnips and sweat for a few minutes. Stir in the stock, cover and simmer for 20 minutes. Blend the soup with a stick blender until smooth, then stir in the cream and horseradish. Season the soup with salt, pepper and cayenne pepper.

Cut the brioche bun into cubes. Wash the thyme, pat dry and pick off the leaves. Heat the clarified butter in a frying pan. Briefly fry the brioche cubes. Stir in the thyme and fry the croutons until crunchy. Season with salt and pepper.

Divide the hot soup among four bowls and serve garnished with the croutons.

SERVES 4

1 large French shallot

500 g (1 lb 2 oz) parsnips

1 tbsp olive oil

4 cups (1 litre) vegetable stock

100 ml (3½ fl oz) single (pure) cream

3 tsp bottled horseradish

Salt

Pepper

1 pinch cayenne pepper

200 g (7 oz) brioche bun

4 sprigs thyme

2 tbsp clarified butter

INDEX OF INGREDIENTS

INDEX OF RECIPES

PHOTOGRAPHY

Julia Stix hails from Vienna. Having working with the daily newspaper *Die Presse* for a few years, she is now a freelance photographer. She is also a passionate cook and loves showing food off in all of its delicious glory. Julia has been in charge of the photography for numerous cookbooks. She publishes her work regularly in Austrian and international magazines.

FOOD STYLING

Eva Fischer studied health management in Austria. She is a trained food photographer and stylist, food blogger, diet coach and recipe developer. Eva's popular blog at www.foodtastic.at has received multiple awards.

Published in 2021 by Murdoch Books, an imprint of Allen & Unwin
First published in 2020 by Hölker Verlag

Murdoch Books Australia
83 Alexander Street
Crows Nest NSW 2065
Phone: +61 (0) 2 8425 0100
murdochbooks.com.au
info@murdochbooks.com.au

Murdoch Books UK
Ormond House
26–27 Boswell Street
London WC1N 3JZ
Phone: +44 (0) 20 8785 5995
murdochbooks.co.uk
info@murdochbooks.co.uk

For corporate orders & custom publishing, contact our business development team at
salesenquiries@murdochbooks.com.au

Food photography: Julia Stix
Food styling: Eva Fischer
Layout and typesetting: Stefanie Wawer
Editor: Jasmin Parapatits
Production: Anja Bergmann
Poem: Joseph von Eichendorff, Weihnachten/Christmas
Lithography: FSM Premedia GmbH & Co. KG, Munster

Publisher: Corinne Roberts
Cover design: Estee Sarsfield
Translator: Claudia McQuillan-Koch (recipes); Christopher Newton (poem)
English-language editor: Justine Harding

Cover Design © Murdoch Books 2021
Text © Hölker Verlag in Coppenrath Verlag GmbH & Co. KG, Hafenweg 30, 48155 Münster, Germany

ISBN 9 781 92235 185 2 Australia
ISBN 9 781 91166 834 3 UK

A catalogue record for this
book is available from the
National Library of Australia

A catalogue record for this book is available from the British Library

Printed and bound in China by C&C Offset Printing Co., Ltd.

OVEN GUIDE: You may find cooking times vary depending on the oven you are using. For fan-forced ovens,
as a general rule, set the oven temperature to 20°C (70°F) lower than indicated in the recipe.

TABLESPOON MEASURES: We have used 15 ml (3 teaspoon) tablespoon measures. If you are using a larger
Australian 20 ml (4 teaspoon) tablespoon, use 1 teaspoon less of the ingredient for each tablespoon specified.

10 9 8 7 6 5 4 3 2 1